S0-AUT-118

A gift for

From

Tiny Tidings of Joy

for You, Daughter

Illustrations by Amy Rosenberg

COUNTRYMAN

Babbling Brook
Little Works of Heart

Published by J. Countryman,
a division of Thomas Nelson, Inc.,
Nashville, Tennessee 37214

Project Editor: Terri Gibbs

Designed by Left Coast Design Inc.,
Portland, Oregon

ISBN: 08499-9671-6

www.jcountryman.com

Printed in Singapore

A tiny tiding
sent to say,
"A daughter like you
brings joy
to each day!"

How shall we
go about warming
the cold
December chill?

We'll think of the
gift of each new day
and spread
abundant good will!

To me
you will always be
the STAR!!!

Let me tell you just how special I think you are:

_____

_____

_____

_____

_____

_____

_____

_____

Candy canes of
white and red,
sugar-plums dancing
in your head,
'tis the season for joy
and laughter,
and memories to keep
for ever after.

A friendly
smile
can warm
the coldest day.

Every gift
given in
love...

is given
well.

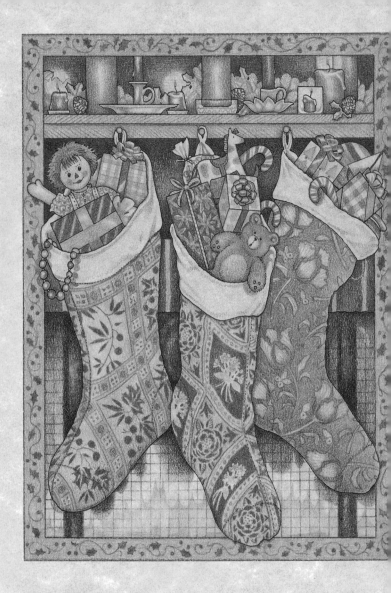

If I could fill your stocking
with any gift at all,
I'd fill it with the gift of:

_____

_____

_____

_____

_____

_____

_____

_____

The gifts God gives
are sometimes small,
but they're sent
with love,
so treasure them all.

A little Christmas prayer for you:

_____

_____

_____

_____

_____

_____

_____

_____

_____

_____

_____

The snow falls white
so bright and clear,
like an angel
announcing
this blessed
time of year.

Peace on Earth!

Not all the gifts
are under
the tree . . .

for you are one of
the best gifts
ever given to me.

Wishing
you sweet
joy and cheer,
not just at
Christmas
but every day
of the year!

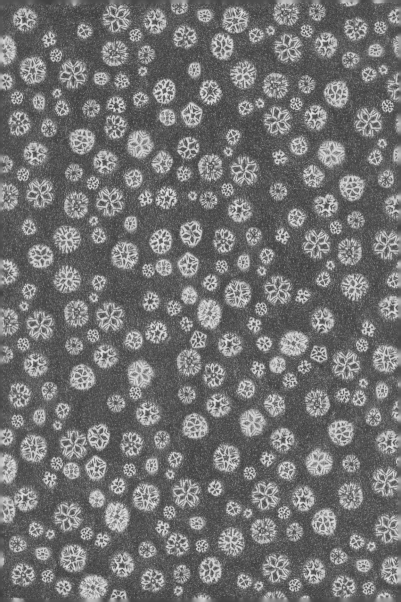